# 28:19

## THE SKILLS FOR DISCIPLE-MAKING
### Participant Manual

## ROB FISCHER

28:19
THE SKILLS FOR DISCIPLE-MAKING
Participant Manual

© 2015 Rob Fischer

ISBN-13:978-1511436755

# TABLE OF CONTENTS

# HOW TO USE THIS MANUAL

*This Participant Manual serves as a companion to the book 28:19 – The Skills for Disciple-Making.*

## What are the Skills for Disciple-Making?

*The Skills for Disciple-Making* are relational skills that equip followers of Jesus in propelling themselves and others forward in their relationship with God. *The Skills for Disciple-Making* are biblical, relational, transferable skills for making disciples of Jesus Christ. We present these skills in a thirteen-week format that is conducive for use in both large or small groups. This experience includes both personal projects and small group discussion elements and simulations.

## Goal

The goal of *The Skills for Disciple-Making* is an ever-deepening relationship with Christ that results in life change—life change in you and in others whom you lead, interact with, and influence.

## How to Use this Manual

I've designed this Training Manual for use with a spiritual partner, a small group, or a large group with a small group element. Due to the nature of much of this work, please be sensitive to the fact that many of the exercises, role-plays and simulations are specifically designed for same-gender pairs or small groups. The reasons for this are for effectiveness and propriety.

There are two types of pre-work to complete before each session: 1) Individual reading in the 28:19 book; and, 2) Projects listed in this *Participant Manual*. (Note: if you're using this Participant Manual, use the discussion questions in this manual and ignore the questions in the book.)

The weekly group meetings are the Modeling and Coaching Sessions described in this manual and follow the pre-work for each session. For this reason, this Participant Manual is not designed for personal study and would be ineffective in that application. The Skills for Disciple-Making must be practiced, modeled and coached in the context of relationships with others.

You will need at least 90 minutes per group session to adequately work through the material and exercises. Make every attempt to approach each session from a practical, real-life perspective. The goal of 28:19 is not learning "stuff," but growing deeper in Christ and experiencing His transforming power.

If you are a facilitator for *The Skills for Disciple-Making* experience, you will play a different role depending on the nature of the group you're leading. If you are simply entering into a spiritual partnership with one or more same gender individuals, or if you're leading a small group of individuals, you may find yourself initiating discussions, but your relationship with the other members should be mutual and reciprocal. Your job is to manage the process and time and to be a facilitator and an equal member, not a teacher.

If you are leading a large group that is split into small groups, you will work as a facilitator to welcome and initially engage the whole large group, facilitate some discussion, launch the small group time, and then call the small groups back together into the large group at the end of each session. Each of the small groups within the large group should be self-led. The large group facilitator should participate in one of the small groups.

Whether you are a large or small group facilitator, look over the questions and exercises in the Modeling and Coaching Sessions before each session. Decide which questions to discuss as a large group, and which to confine to a small group. Some of the questions and exercises are specifically designed for same gender partners. I've provided tips for each session as to what I would recommend.

If you are facilitating a large group with small group breakouts, allow the small groups to pray with each other at the end and then call the small groups back together into the large group and go over the assignments for the next week. Remember, your role is as a facilitator and not a teacher.

The last two-thirds of this Participant Manual contain numerous simulations and role-plays. *Please do not underestimate the importance and power of practicing all of these aloud with each other*. If you've ever taken a CPR course, you know that you cannot pass the course without working on Resusci Anne. Similarly, commercial pilots don't take the controls of a jet loaded with passengers until they've spent significant time in the simulators. Consider these simulations and role plays in the same way. The role-plays are vital to learning these disciple-making skills!

**Your approach to *28:19 – The Skills for Disciple-Making***

As you embark on this experience, invite and expect God to change you. The pre-work, simulations, role-plays, projects, questions, and discussions are all designed to move you into proximity with Jesus Christ, so please work them diligently! And as you draw near to Christ, you cannot remain unchanged! The exciting thing is that as Jesus changes you, He uses you to impact, influence, and change others around you.

Also, please tackle the reading and personal projects early in the week or you'll find yourself running out of time to complete them. And, if you work on the projects early in the week, the Holy Spirit will ruminate in you throughout the week about what He wants to teach you. The first three chapters are the longest, due to their foundational nature, so stay with it!

I mentioned role-plays and simulations. Please **do not skip** over these or minimize their impact! The simulations you'll encounter here are necessary to practice the skills of discipling others. Have fun with the role-plays and simulations! Ham it up and enjoy throwing yourself into character. I can almost guarantee that God will use these role-plays and simulations to draw you closer to Him in some very unexpected and unusual ways. This nearly always happens.

One more thing on the role-plays and simulations—sometimes we'll ask you to pray for someone in a simulated situation. That strikes some people as phony, hokey, or irreverent, but Jesus Himself dispels that myth. In Luke 11:1-4, Jesus was praying and His disciples were observing Him. When He finished, they asked, "Lord, teach us to pray." In response, Jesus said, "Pray like this..." (Matthew 6:9 NLT) and then He modeled what we call the Lord's Prayer for them. Jesus led the way, so it's okay for us to model or simulate a prayer with others like He did.

## Learning objectives

Upon completion of this training and practices the participant will be able to:

1. Model Christ's transforming power!
   a. By enjoying God
   b. By abiding in Christ
   c. By obeying Christ
   d. By partnering with other followers

2. Unleash a vision of God for others!
   a. Through your story
   b. Through His Word
   c. Through prayer
   d. Through His works

3. Courageously challenge others toward Christ!
   a. By applying God's Word
   b. By taking them to God in prayer
   c. By placing a "Y" in their path
   d. By celebrating their personal victories

# INTRODUCTORY SESSION

**To prepare for this session:**

1. Read the Foreword and Introduction in the book, *28:19 – The Skills for Disciple-Making.*

2. Respond to the questions below as thoughtfully and candidly as you can.

   a. Identify at least three insights about discipleship that Rob discussed that you found particularly impactful.

   b. What was your greatest "Aha!" from this chapter?

   c. Reflect back over your life. Who have been the individuals who have most significantly propelled you forward in your relationship with Christ? What did those individuals do that was so impactful for you?

   d. What is the extent of your experience in discipling others in their relationship with Christ?

e.  What is God currently doing in your life? What areas of your life is He changing? What has He been speaking to you about? In what ways are you growing in your relationship with Him? What is He teaching you from His Word?

3.  What is the current, most pressing need in your personal discipleship process in becoming more like Jesus?

4.  Make five copies of the *Lifestyle Benchmark* (at the back of this manual or download and email from the following link: *http://fischerleadershipcoaching.com/robs-books/free-tools/*). Keep one copy to complete on yourself and give the other four copies to four people who know you well. Ask those individuals to complete the Benchmark for you and to return it to you anonymously. Please make every effort to maintain the anonymity of each respondent. A good way to do this is to give them an unmarked envelope in which they can insert the *Lifestyle Benchmark* and seal it. Hold on to these returned, unopened *Lifestyle Benchmarks* until the fifth session (Chapter 4) on spiritual partnership.

## Group Session: Modeling and Coaching

This is the time you spend each week with whomever you are going through this Participant Manual (i.e., a spiritual partner, a small group, or a large group). If you are meeting as a large group with a small group element, please refer to the Tips in the box.

1. Open in prayer thanking the Lord for His presence among you. Pray expecting God to work in your midst and invite Him to continue to change you making you more like Christ.

2. Take a few minutes to get to know each other with brief introductions: (E.g., name, family, occupation and what they would like to take away from the *28:19* experience.)

> **Tips:** If you are meeting as a large group with a small group element, I suggest that you work through the first five items below as a large group and then break into small groups for question 6. Then call everyone back to the large group for items 7-9.

3. If you're leading a group, we recommend that you have the group establish "ground rules" by which they'll abide to help things run smoothly. I always "prime the pump" by suggesting one or two and let the group come up with the rest. (Some of these "ground rules" may include: Starting and stopping on time, confidentiality, doing the work, etc.)

4. Briefly walk through this manual to become familiar with and understand how it's laid out. Notice that there are projects to complete prior to each session and then instructions on how to conduct each session. **Point out that there are discussion questions in the book, but we will ignore those and only work the ones in the Participant Manual.**

5.  Explain the practice of praying for each other "on the spot." In other words, if someone asks for prayer or even voices a need that warrants prayer, stop and ask if someone would pray for that need "on the spot." After you pray, explain that "praying on the spot" is one of the habits we want to model for each other in *28:19*.

6.  Discuss the Pre-work questions that focus on the Introduction from the book.

7.  Go over conversational prayer guidelines. The guidelines below are designed to help us pray with each other *conversationally.*

    ■ Pray *short*, phrase or sentence prayers (Don't hog the conversation!)

    ■ Listen to the Holy Spirit and each other

    ■ Piggyback on each other's prayers. Stay on a theme until it seems right to move on

    ■ Keep your prayers vertical (God-ward)

    ■ Embrace silence as an opportunity to listen to God, transition to another topic, or process what has been prayed

    ■ Believe the best of each other

8.  Remind everyone to make five copies of the *Lifestyle Benchmark* (at the back of this manual or download and email from the following link: *http://fischerleadership-coaching.com/robs-books/free-tools/*). Keep one copy to complete on yourself and give the other four copies to

four people who know you well. Ask those individuals to complete the Benchmark for you and to return it to you anonymously. Please make every effort to maintain the anonymity of each respondent. A good way to do this is to give them an unmarked envelope in which they can insert the *Lifestyle Benchmark* and seal it. Hold on to these returned, unopened *Lifestyle Benchmarks* until the fifth session (Chapter 4) on spiritual partnership.

9. Briefly go over the expectations for next week and rehearse the logistics of where and when to meet.

# Model Christ's Transforming Power by Enjoying God!

**To prepare for this session:**

1. Read chapter 1 in *28:19 – The Skills for Disciple-Making* book.

2. Memorize Psalm 73:25 and meditate on it during the week.

3. Spend an hour in solitude with God this week. Find some-place away from people and distractions. Refer back to this chapter in the book on how to cultivate your enjoy-ment of God. Record your experience with God here. In what ways did you enjoy Him? How did you express your enjoyment of Him? If He spoke to you, what did He say? How do you know when the Lord is speaking to you?

4. Respond to the following questions:
   a. What story or example impacted you most in this chapter and why?

b.  Why is our enjoyment of God so crucial for our spiritual transformation?

c.  To what extent does your life currently model Christ's transforming power? What is hindering you or holding you back in this regard?

d.  How comfortable do you feel with boldly urging others to follow you as you follow Christ, as Paul did? If you're uncomfortable doing this, to what do you attribute your discomfort?

e.  To what extent would you describe your spiritual transformation as having an upward "trajectory"? Read 2 Peter 1:3-9. (To what degree are you experiencing Christ's transforming power "in increasing measure"?) Talk to God and ask Him to continue to change you and make you more like Him.

f.  How new for you is the concept of enjoying God? How comfortable are you with this concept? If you are uncomfortable with it, what is the cause of your discomfort?

g.  To what extent does your life model Christ's transforming power by *enjoying God*? In what ways have you enjoyed and delighted in God recently? Tell someone else before the next group session something you enjoy about God.

## Group Session: Modeling and Coaching

This is the time you spend each week with whomever you are going through this Participant Manual (i.e., a spiritual partner, a small group, or a large group). If you are meeting as a large group with a small group element, please refer to the Tips in the box.

> **Tips:** You may want to work through the first three items below as a large group and then break into small groups for the remaining items 4-7. Then bring the large group back for number 8.

By practicing the skills presented here you will model and coach each other in those skills with the goal of propelling each other into deeper relationship with Jesus Christ, resulting in a changed life. When you meet together:

1.  Open in prayer thanking the Lord for His presence among you. Pray expecting God to work in your midst and invite Him to continue to change you making you more like Christ.

2.  Be attentive to opportunities to pray for each other on the spot.

3.  Ask, "In what ways has God revealed Himself to you recently?"

4.  In your small groups, discuss your responses to the questions you prepared for this session. Quote Psalm 73:25 for each other and tell what the Lord revealed as a result of meditating on this verse.

5. Have each person share about their experience spending an hour with the Lord in solitude. In what ways did you enjoy the Lord? How did you express your enjoyment of Him? If He spoke to you, what did He say? How do you know when the Lord is speaking to you?

6. As you rehearsed these Projects with each other, draw attention to specific individuals who *modeled the enjoyment of God* for you in this session. Detail for them in what ways they did this for you.

7. Spend time praying together conversationally. Focus primarily on the topic of this session and how Christ wants to change you. The guidelines below are designed to help us pray with each other *conversationally*.

   - Pray short, phrase or sentence prayers (Don't hog the conversation!)

   - Listen to the Holy Spirit and each other

   - Piggyback on each other's prayers. Stay on a theme until it seems right to move on

   - Keep your prayers vertical (God-ward)

   - Embrace silence as an opportunity to listen to God, transition to another topic, or process what has been prayed

   - Believe the best of each other

8. Briefly go over the expectations for next week.

# Model Christ's Transforming Power by Abiding in Christ!

**To prepare for this session:**

1. Read chapter 2 in *28:19 – The Skills for Disciple-Making* book.

2. Memorize John 15:5 and meditate on it this week.

3. Respond to the following questions:

   a. What was your greatest "Aha!" from this chapter?

   b. Keeping the metaphor of the vine and branches fresh in your mind all week, *practice abiding in Christ* throughout each day. Stay conscious of your dependence on Christ for everything. Focus your attention on Him and allow Him to produce His "fruit" (His character and its resultant thoughts, attitudes, words and behaviors). Let Him work in and through you. Record here any special insights and experiences during the week.

c.  In what ways do you know Christ better today than you did a year ago? Where do you see Him active in your life? What following skills do you practice in order to know Him better? How do you respond to Him when things don't go well? How does all this relate to abiding in Him?

d.  To what extent do you find yourself compartmentalizing your life? (That is, living by differing standards depending on the "compartment" you are in at a given time.) Why is compartmentalized living so dangerous? What can you do to avoid and prevent compartmentalizing your life?

## Group Session: Modeling and Coaching

This is the time you spend each week with whomever you are going through this Participant Manual (i.e., a spiritual partner, a small group, or a large group). If you are meeting as a large group with a small group element, please refer to the Tips in the box.

By practicing the skills presented here you will model and coach each other in those skills with the goal of propelling each other into deeper relationship with Jesus Christ, resulting in a changed life. When you meet together:

> **Tips:** Work through the first three questions below as a whole group; then break up into gender-specific pairs for question 4; conduct questions 5-8 in small groups; and then back to the large group for question 9.

1. Open in prayer thanking the Lord for His presence among you. Pray expecting God to work in your midst and invite Him to continue to change you making you more like Christ.

2. Be attentive to opportunities to pray for each other and pray on the spot.

3. Model the *Abiding Illustration* for the group as described in the book. Use props and refer to John 15:5 and Galatians 5:22-23.

4. Pair up men with men and women with women and take turns demonstrating the Abiding Illustration with each other right now. In this simulation, assume that each of you has a problem with outbursts of anger. Be sure to use props to represent the vine, branch and fruit and refer to John 15:5 and Galatians 5:22-23. (This will take about 15 minutes.)

5. In your small groups ask, "In what ways were you able to abide in Christ this past week?"

6. In your small group, discuss your responses to the questions you prepared for this session and quote John 15:5 for each other.

7. Share with each other how a member of your group has personally modeled Christ's transforming power for you by abiding in Christ. (Maybe this is something they shared or did in this session or in another context.)

8. Spend time praying together conversationally. Focus primarily on the topic of this session and how Christ wants to change you. The guidelines below are designed to help us pray with each other *conversationally*.

   ■ Pray short, phrase or sentence prayers
     (Don't hog the conversation!)

   ■ Listen to the Holy Spirit and each other

   ■ Piggyback on each other's prayers. Stay on a theme until it seems right to move on

- Keep your prayers vertical (God-ward)

- Embrace silence as an opportunity to listen to God, transition to another topic, or process what has been prayed

- Believe the best of each other

9. Briefly go over the expectations for next week.

# Model Christ's Transforming Power by Obeying Christ!

**To prepare for this session:**

1. Read chapter 3 in *28:19 – The Skills for Disciple-Making* book.

2. Respond to the following questions and share the abiding illustration:

   a. Memorize John 14:15 and meditate on it this week.

   b. Before the next session, share the Abiding Illustration with someone. Be sure to use props (e.g., knife, fork, and coffee mug, etc.) for the vine, branch, and fruit and refer to both John 15:5 and Galatians 5:22-23. Also, don't worry about finding "the right situation" in which to share the *Abiding Illustration*. Share this illustration with your spouse, a close friend, a child, anybody will do! Simply tell them that you have an assignment and would like to show them something. Record your experience here and don't be surprised if God uses this exercise in someone's life profoundly!

3. What specific area or areas of your life do you struggle with submitting to Christ's leadership? (This is merely another way of looking at sin in our lives.) Why do you think you struggle with those areas? What do you fear you would lose by submitting to Christ in those areas? For the child of God, fear invariably arises out of wrong views of God's character. What misconceptions about God can you expose in your life that might lead to such fears? Search the Scriptures to counter those misconceptions about God.

4. Interact with Rob's statement, "Think of obedience to Christ as more of a lifestyle of submission to Him rather than a set of isolated defining moments."

5. Think of a situation in your own life, similar to Rob's experience behind the wheel. What particular behavior, attitude, or thought pattern would you like Christ to transform in you? Using the four-step process in the book begin the dealing with this sin.

6. What role do following skills like: reading and studying the Word, prayer, solitude, spiritual partnership, etc. play in our obedience to Christ? How do you engage following skills to assist you in obeying Christ?

7. Why does mere "sin avoidance" fall short of the holy living that God desires for us? How do we cultivate a life of holiness?

8. Why must we not think of obedience to Christ in terms of "rule-keeping"? What does it mean to obey Christ?

9. Explain the role of both *dependence* and *diligence* in following and obeying Christ. (See 2 Peter 1:3-9.) Think of an example of how you practice dependent-diligence in your own life.

10. What do we mean by *spiritual trajectory*? Are you on a trajectory of life change in Jesus Christ? What are the evidences of your trajectory? Would others corroborate your self-evaluation?

## Group Session: Modeling and Coaching

This is the time you spend each week with whomever you are going through this Participant Manual (i.e., a spiritual partner, a small group, or a large group). If you are meeting as a large group with a small group element, please refer to the Tips in the box.

**Tips:** Lead the whole group through questions 1-3; then conduct questions 4-6 in small groups; bring everyone back together to address item 7.

By practicing the skills presented here you will model and coach each other in those skills with the goal of propelling each other into deeper relationship with Jesus Christ, resulting in a changed life. When you meet together:

1.  Open in prayer thanking the Lord for His presence among you. Pray expecting God to work in your midst and invite Him to continue to change you making you more like Christ.

2.  Be attentive to opportunities to pray for each other and pray on the spot.

3.  Share with each other what happened as you shared the Abiding Illustration with someone this week.

4.  Discuss your responses to the questions you prepared for this session and quote John 14:15 for each other.

5.  Discuss how this group of Christ-followers can help each other obey Christ. Share with each other how a member of your group (or someone else) has personally modeled Christ's transforming power for you by obeying Christ. (Maybe this is something they shared or did in this session or in another context.)

6.  Spend time praying together conversationally. Focus primarily on the topic of this session and how Christ wants to change you. The guidelines below are designed to help us pray with each other *conversationally*.

    ■ Pray short, phrase or sentence prayers
      (Don't hog the conversation!)

    ■ Listen to the Holy Spirit and each other

    ■ Piggyback on each other's prayers. Stay on a theme until it seems right to move on

    ■ Keep your prayers vertical (God-ward)

    ■ Embrace silence as an opportunity to listen to God, transition to another topic, or process what has been prayed

    ■ Believe the best of each other

7.  Briefly go over the expectations for next week and remember to bring completed Lifestyle Benchmarks.

# Model Christ's Transforming Power by Partnering with Other Followers of Christ!

## To prepare for this session:

1.  Read chapter 4 in *28:19 – The Skills for Disciple-Making* book.

2.  Memorize Proverbs 27:17 and meditate on it this week.

3.  Bring your returned *Lifestyle Benchmarks* unopened.

4.  Beginning this week and throughout the rest of this training, you will have specific projects and opportunities in which to cultivate a "comrades-in-arms" or spiritual partnership. In your next session you will be asked to team up with another same-gender individual who is also currently participating in 28:19. Pray, asking God to prepare you for this "comrades in arms" relationship and expect Him to work in and through you both.

5.  Respond to the following questions:
    a.  What was your biggest "Aha" from this chapter in the book?

b. Discuss the statement, "A 'comrades-in-arms' or spiritual partnership with others will propel us forward in becoming more like Christ."

c. What gets in the way in your life from having a spiritual partner?

d. Think back over the time that you've been following Jesus Christ. What individuals have had a significant impact in your life through their example of following Christ? In what ways have their lives impacted you most?

## Group Session: Modeling and Coaching

This is the time you spend each week with whomever you are going through this Participant Manual (i.e., a spiritual partner, a small group, or a large group). If you are meeting as a large group with a small group element, please refer to the Tips in the box.

By practicing the skills presented here you will model and coach each other in those skills with the goal of propelling each other into deeper relationship with Jesus Christ, resulting in a changed life. When you meet together:

1. Open in prayer thanking the Lord for His presence among you. Pray expecting God to work in your midst and invite Him to continue to change you making you more like Christ.

> **Tips:** address items 1 and 2 with the whole group; then introduce the Lifestyle Benchmark exercise in item 3 and have them do this on their own; conduct questions 4-7 in small groups; then have them pair off in gender-specific pairs for question 8 (allow at least 30 minutes for this paired exercise); then gather again into small groups for questions 9-10; and conduct question 11 with the whole group.

2. Be attentive to opportunities to pray for each other and pray on the spot.

1. Open your *Lifestyle Benchmarks* and review them by yourself. Allow a few minutes for this exercise and read through the explanation below aloud.

One of the ways God changes us is through input from others. The *Lifestyle Benchmark* provides us with a unique opportunity to receive feedback from others who know us. Consider their feedback a rare gift from God. Please prayerfully and humbly prepare yourself for receiving this feedback.

You may find some of the feedback shocking or merely confirming. Look for patterns in the feedback rather than anomalies. Please avoid trying to figure out who wrote what. Instead, invite God to put His finger on one or more areas of your life and let Him begin to change you.

Questions to ask yourself: What area(s) of my life is God speaking to me about transforming? Does the *Lifestyle Benchmark* reveal an area in my life on which Christ would like to work?

The *Lifestyle Benchmarks* are for your eyes only unless you choose to share the results with your group or a spiritual partner (which I would encourage you to do).

2.  You're not expected to do so, but is there anything that anyone would like to share with the small group as a result of the *Lifestyle Benchmark* exercise?

3.  Recite Proverbs 27:17 for each other.

4.  Briefly review your responses to the questions you answered in preparation for this week.

5. Review the five characteristics of spiritual partnerships from this chapter. Which one or ones do you find most challenging? Pick one of these characteristics and explain why you think it's so important for spiritual partnerships. How will you personally display that characteristic?

6. Beginning this week and throughout the rest of 28:19 we ask that you team up with another same-gender person to serve as a spiritual partner. (If you have an odd number of individuals, feel free to create a triad instead of a pair, but always make the partnerships gender-specific.) Break up into those pairs now and in your pairs follow the instructions below:

    a. Verbally agree to maintain confidentiality with each other. What's said here stays here. Also, grant each other permission to "ask tough questions" and to speak into one another's lives.

    b. Ask each other and respond to the question, "What is your greatest area of challenge right now in your walk with Christ?" (Don't try to "fix" each other, instead listen intently.)

    c. As each of you responds to the above question, ask: "What do you think God wants you to do regarding this challenge?" Again, listen to each other's response. If they feel stuck, offer to brainstorm a solution with them.

    d. When you each agree to a plan of action for moving forward in Christ regarding this challenge, ask each other: "How committed are you to following through with what you said you'd do?" Then ask, "How would you like to be held accountable?"

e. Pray with and for each other, calling on the Lord to help you follow through with what you said you'd do.

f. Exchange phone numbers so you can contact each other during the week.

7. Come back together as a small group and debrief the previous exercise, while maintaining confidentiality. What you just experienced was a taste of spiritual partnership. What did you learn from the exercise? To what extent did you experience "transformational relationship" in the context of this spiritual partnership? How effective was it?

8. Spend time praying together conversationally. Focus primarily on the topic of this session and how Christ wants to change you. The guidelines below are designed to help us pray with each other *conversationally*.

■ Pray short, phrase or sentence prayers (Don't hog the conversation!)

■ Listen to the Holy Spirit and each other

■ Piggyback on each other's prayers. Stay on a theme until it seems right to move on

■ Keep your prayers vertical (God-ward)

■ Embrace silence as an opportunity to listen to God, transition to another topic, or process what has been prayed

■ Believe the best of each other

9. Briefly go over the assignments for next week.

# CHAPTER 5

# Unleash a Vision of God through Your Story!

## To prepare for this session:

1. Read chapter 5 in *28:19 – The Skills for Disciple-Making* book.

2. Memorize Luke 8:38-39 and meditate on it this week.

3. What was your biggest "Aha" in reading this chapter in the book?

4. Write a fresh story of God's work in your life that will unleash a vision of God for others. Armed with that story or some other fresh work of God in your life, initiate the opportunity to unleash a vision of God for two different people this week. Find room to write your story on page 107 in this manual.

   You can be as subtle as taking advantage of a situation that warrants your story; to casually asking someone, "Hey, can I share with you what God has been doing in my life lately?" Or in a totally non-subtle way, simply ask, "I'm going through a course right now and have an assignment to share a fresh story of what God is doing in my life.

Would you mind if I shared that with you?" The point is, don't wait "for the perfect moment!" Make it happen!

5. Consider the impact of your two experiences. In what ways were you able to unleash a vision of God as you unleashed a vision of Him to others through your story? What impact did unleashing a vision of God through your story have on others? What impact did this action have on you?

## Group Session: Modeling and Coaching

This is the time you spend each week with whomever you are going through this Participant Manual (i.e., a spiritual partner, a small group, or a large group). If you are meeting as a large group with a small group element, please refer to the Tips in the box.

By practicing the skills presented here you will model and coach each other in those skills with the goal of propelling each other into deeper relationship with Jesus Christ, resulting in a changed life. When you meet together:

**Tips:** Work through the first three items below as a whole group; then break into your spiritual partnerships for question 4 (allow at least 15-20 minutes for this exercise); reconvene in small groups for items 5-7; then bring everyone together for item 8.

1. Open in prayer thanking the Lord for His presence among you. Pray expecting God to work in your midst and invite Him to continue to change you making you more like Christ.

2. Be attentive to opportunities to pray for each other and pray on the spot.

3. There were two simulations in the book that are reprinted below. Please have two volunteers role-play these one at a time with a short debrief between simulations.

## Simulation one

| | |
|---|---|
| Bob | "I don't know what's going on lately, but I'm really struggling with trusting God in my life." |
| Drew | "I understand exactly how you feel. All of us from time to time experience emotions like that. So don't sweat it! Hey, I was going to ask you, what did you think of that game the other night?" |

## Simulation one debrief

Discuss what Drew did and didn't do in this simulation. How effective was Drew in assisting his friend Bob? If you were Bob, how would Drew's comments impact you?

## Simulation two

| | |
|---|---|
| Bob | "I don't know what's going on lately, but I'm really struggling with trusting God in my life." |
| Drew | "What specifically are you struggling with?" |
| Bob | "Does God really answer prayers? I feel like I pray and nothing happens." |
| Drew | "There are times when I feel the same way you do right now, but to answer your question, yes! God does answer prayer! Let me share something that happened just the other day. My wife and I were traveling to Anchorage, Alaska and needed a car for a few days, but we didn't have the money to rent one. We prayed asking God to provide for us and the same day a friend emailed |

us and offered us the use of his truck! We hadn't even mentioned our need to this friend. God does love us and He answers prayer!"

## Simulation two debrief

What was the difference between the two simulations? Think about how both simulations impacted you. How did Drew unleash a vision of God for Bob? If you were Bob, what effect would Drew have had on you in this second simulation?

4. Break up into your spiritual partnerships and share with each other the fresh story of God's work in your life that you prepared for today. Then, discuss with each other how God used each other's stories to unleash a vision of Him for you. (Note: If your spiritual partner is absent, then partner with another same-gender person or turn a two-some into a three-some.)

5. Come back together in your small groups. Share what happened when you shared your fresh story of God's work in your life with two people this past week.

6. Transition to your responses to any of the other questions you worked on prior to this session. Quote Luke 8:38-39 for each other and ask each other what the Lord revealed to you as a result of meditating on this verse.

7. Pray for each other using the guidelines for *conversational prayer:*

   ▪ Pray short, phrase or sentence prayers (Don't hog the conversation!)

   ▪ Listen to the Holy Spirit and each other

   ▪ Piggyback on each other's prayers. Stay on a theme until it seems right to move on

   ▪ Keep your prayers vertical (God-ward)

   ▪ Embrace silence as an opportunity to listen to God, transition to another topic, or process what has been prayed

   ▪ Believe the best of each other

8. Briefly go over the assignments for next week.

# Unleash a Vision of God through His Word!

**To prepare for this session:**

1. Read chapter 6 in *28:19 – The Skills for Disciple-Making* book.

2. Memorize Psalm 130:5 and meditate on it this week.

3. As you've read God's Word this week, in what ways has He unleashed a vision of Himself to you?

4. Apply the Equipped in God's Word model to Luke 11:1-4, working through all four phases of the model. Remember to go to the Word with the expectation of meeting with God. Ask Him for a fresh word from Him. Find room to work through Luke 11:1-4 on page 109 in this manual.

5. Armed with a "fresh word" from God from Luke 11:1-4, look for and take advantage of an opportunity to unleash a vision of God for someone from the Word using that passage. If no opportunity happens to present itself, take the initiative to unleash a vision of God from His Word in someone's life simply for the enjoyment of sharing this truth with them. Record here what happens.

## Group Session: Modeling and Coaching

This is the time you spend each week with whomever you are going through this Participant Manual (i.e., a spiritual partner, a small group, or a large group). If you are meeting as a large group with a small group element, please refer to the Tips in the box.

By practicing the skills presented here you will model and coach each other in those skills with the goal of propelling each other into deeper relationship with Jesus Christ, resulting in a changed life. When you meet together:

> **Tips:** Address questions 1-3 as a whole group (use the appropriate gender simulation depending on the makeup of your group); conduct questions 4-6 in small groups; for questions 7-8 break into your spiritual partnerships (allow at least 20 minutes for these exercises); reconvene the whole group for item 9.

1. Open in prayer thanking the Lord for His presence among you. Pray expecting God to work in your midst and invite Him to continue to change you making you more like Christ.

2. Be attentive to opportunities to pray for each other on the spot.

3. Below is a simulation that you read in the book for this chapter. Please ask two volunteers to role-play this simulation and then debrief it. (There is a simulation for women and one for men.)

## Women's Simulation

Angela and Rachel are both followers of Christ and close friends. Rachel called Angela and asked if they could meet together. They've both just arrived at a coffee house.

Rachel     "Hi, Angela (they hug). Thank you so much for taking time to meet with me."

Angela     "Rachel, it's my pleasure! You sounded pretty distraught over the phone. What's going on?"

Rachel     "Chad doesn't seem to be any closer to receiving Christ today than he was three years ago, when I gave my life to Christ. Our lives seem so separate and so distant. It's almost as though my coming to Christ has driven us further apart! Chad even said so the other night after we had an argument."

Angela     "Rachel, I know this is really difficult! I went through the same thing with John for eight years until he finally caved and surrendered to Christ."

Rachel     "Wow! Eight years! (*despairingly*) I don't think I can live with Chad like this for another five years." (*tears flowing and Angela embraces her again*)

Angela     "You know, I was reading in 1 Timothy this morning and ran across some verses that I think will give you hope." (*Angela pulls out a New Testament and starts flipping through the pages.*) "Here it is. It's 1 Timothy 1, starting with verse 12, Paul is writing:

*I thank Christ Jesus our Lord, who has given me strength to do His work. He considered me trustworthy and appointed me to serve Him, even though I used to blaspheme the name of Christ. In my insolence, I persecuted His people. But God had mercy on me because I did it in ignorance and unbelief. Oh, how generous and gracious our Lord was! He filled me with the faith and love that come from Christ Jesus.*

*This is a trustworthy saying, and everyone should accept it: "Christ Jesus came into the world to save sinners"—and I am the worst of them all. But God had mercy on me so that Christ Jesus could use me as a prime example of His great patience with even the worst sinners. Then others will realize that they, too, can believe in Him and receive eternal life. (NLT)*

Rachel, think of it! Paul calls himself the worst of sinners. He was a blasphemer and persecutor of the church and yet Jesus saved him. In fact, Paul was going to Damascus to arrest Christians and throw them in prison when he met Jesus. And look what God did with him! If Paul was the worst of sinners and God worked through him so amazingly, just think what God can do with Chad."

Rachel     "You're right. I hadn't thought of applying Paul's story to Chad. What really gives me hope is that God didn't just save Paul to keep him from doing all that awful stuff. God made him into a man of God. That's what I want for Chad!"

Angela     "Let's pray right now that God would continue to work in Chad's life, drawing him into relationship with Him and transform him into a man of God."

## Women's Simulation Debrief

How did Angela unleash a vision of God for Rachel through God's Word? What made her words so relational and relevant? As you heard the simulation, what impact did this unleashing a vision of God through His Word have on you?

## Men's Simulation

Chad and Jacob have agreed to a comrades-in-arms relationship and meet weekly at a local coffee house.

| | |
|---|---|
| Chad | "Hey, Jacob, how's it going?" |
| Jacob | "It's going alright, and you?" |
| Chad | "I've been better. Heather's cancer is really beginning to take a toll on her." |
| Jacob | "I'm so sorry, Jacob. I can't imagine how difficult this is for you two right now." |
| Chad | "I wish I could take on the cancer and the pain for her, but I can't. I really feel helpless. We've prayed and prayed for her healing. When I open the Bible to read in the morning, my eyes simply glaze over. I can't concentrate." |
| Jacob | "What would you like to see God do in your lives right now?" |
| Chad | "Obviously, to heal Heather. And yet we both have sensed that God is in this thing. We know He cares for us no matter what happens, but it's just so hard! But to answer your question, I'd |

|        | like God to confirm His presence with us and to flood us with His peace." |
|--------|--------|
| Jacob  | "I understand. You know, in my quiet time this morning I read Romans 8 and I think you may find comfort in it. Would you mind if I read the last part of the chapter for you right now?" |
| Chad   | "No, please do." |
| Jacob  | "I'm reading Romans 8:31-39:" |

*What, then, shall we say in response to these things? If God is for us, who can be against us? He who did not spare His own Son, but gave Him up for us all—how will He not also, along with Him, graciously give us all things? Who will bring any charge against those whom God has chosen? It is God who justifies. Who then is the one who condemns? No one. Christ Jesus who died—more than that, who was raised to life—is at the right hand of God and is also interceding for us.*

*Who shall separate us from the love of Christ? Shall trouble or hardship or persecution or famine or nakedness or danger or sword? As it is written: "For Your sake we face death all day long; we are considered as sheep to be slaughtered."*

*No, in all these things we are more than conquerors through Him who loved us. For I am convinced that neither death nor life, neither angels nor demons, neither the present nor the future, nor any powers, neither height nor depth, nor anything else in all creation, will be able to separate us from the love of God that is in Christ Jesus our Lord.*

"This is the passage that the Lord encouraged Cheryl and me with when my dad passed away last year. We were so comforted by the fact that God is bigger than any circumstance or situation!"

Chad    "This is actually one of my favorite passages in the Bible, but I haven't read it in a while. This is good. I see here that God confirms His great love for Heather and me even in the face of our current troubles. Nothing, not even death, can separate us from the love of Christ. I'm reminded too that Jesus is at the right hand of God and is praying for us. That's huge and gives me real peace! Thanks for this reminder."

Jacob    "God is good. I know He will get you guys through this and you know that Cheryl and I are here with you. Let me pray for you…"

## Men's Simulation Debrief

In what way did Jacob unleash a vision of God from His Word for Chad? What made Jacob's words so impactful in Chad's life? As you heard the simulation, what impact did this unleashing a vision of God through His Word have on you?

4.  In your small groups, ask each other, "What has the Lord been revealing to you from His Word lately?"

5.  Quote Psalm 130:5 for each other and ask each other what the Lord revealed to you as a result of meditating on this verse.

6.  Briefly discuss your experience working through the Equipped in God's Word model on Luke 11:1-4. (Leave time to conduct the next exercise.)

7.  Break up into pairs with your spiritual partners. (Note: If your spiritual partner is absent, then partner with another same-gender person or turn a two-some into a three-some.) Take turns role-playing the following situation. Make sure that both of you have an opportunity to play both roles.

    Role A     "Hi, (name), thanks for meeting with me. You often talk about how you pray, listening to and talking with God and I thought you might be able to help me. I'm really struggling with prayer. I'm new at it and just can't get the hang of it. Maybe I'm just not gifted to pray."

    Role B     (Using Luke 11:1-4, unleash a vision of God for this person.)

**Debrief Role-Play**

Describe how your partner unleashed a vision of God for you through the Word. What impact did their unleashing a vision of God have on you?

8.  In your spiritual partnerships, pray for each other using the guidelines for *conversational prayer*:

    ■ Pray short, phrase or sentence prayers
      (Don't hog the conversation!)

    ■ Listen to the Holy Spirit and each other

    ■ Piggyback on each other's prayers. Stay on a theme until it seems right to move on

    ■ Keep your prayers vertical (God-ward)

    ■ Embrace silence as an opportunity to listen to God, transition to another topic, or process what has been prayed

    ■ Believe the best of each other

9.  Briefly go over the assignments for next week.

# CHAPTER 7

## Unleash a Vision of God through Prayer!

**To prepare for this session:**

1. Read chapter 7 in *28:19 – The Skills for Disciple-Making* book.

2. Memorize Ephesians 3:20 and meditate on it this week.

3. What was your biggest "Aha" from reading this chapter?

4. Read Ephesians 3:14-21 as though the Apostle Paul were unleashing a vision of God for you through this prayer. In what ways does this prayer unleash a vision of God for you?

5. While in conversation with others this week, listen for opportunities to pray on the spot for someone, unleashing a vision of God through prayer. Remember to keep your prayers vertical, biblical, and personal! Record here what happens.

## Group Session: Modeling and Coaching

This is the time you spend each week with whomever you are going through this Participant Manual (i.e., a spiritual partner, a small group, or a large group). If you are meeting as a large group with a small group element, please refer to the Tips in the box.

**Tips:** Address items 1-3 as a whole group; conduct items 4-5 in your spiritual partnerships allowing 15-20 minutes for this exercise; come back into small groups for items 6-8; reconvene as a whole group for item 9.

By practicing the skills presented here you will model and coach each other in those skills with the goal of propelling each other into deeper relationship with Jesus Christ, resulting in a changed life. When you meet together:

1. Open in prayer thanking the Lord for His presence among you. Pray expecting God to work in your midst and invite Him to continue to change you making you more like Christ.

2. Be attentive to opportunities to pray for each other on the spot.

3. Below is a simulation that you read in the book in this chapter. Please ask two volunteers to role-play this one at a time with a short debrief between simulations.

## Simulation

*(women can transpose Darla for Dan and Jane for Josh)*

Dan          "Hi, Josh, how's it going?"

Josh     "Honestly? Not too well! Work is the pits right now."

Dan     "I'm sorry to hear that. What's going on?"

Josh     "A former peer of mine was promoted above me and now I report to him. He's very bright and deserved the promotion. But for some reason he feels threatened by me due to our former relationship. As a result, he is constantly talking me down in front of others and slandering my reputation. And he's a total pain to work with. I am doing my job well and my numbers demonstrate that, but you'd never know it by the way he treats me!"

Dan     "I can imagine how tough this situation must be for you! I'm not sure that I have any great advice for you, but may I pray for you right now?"

Josh     "Sure, I would appreciate that!"

Dan     (Dan steps closer to Josh and places a hand on Josh's shoulder.) "Dear Father, thank You that You not only know about everything that Josh is experiencing right now at work, but You also care about him more than we can possibly imagine. Please give Josh your supernatural peace and joy through this ordeal. I pray that You would protect him and his integrity. In spite of what's happening to him, help Josh to continue to represent You well and give him success in his work. Please change his boss' heart and show him that Josh poses no threat to him.

You are the Father of compassion and the God of all comfort, so please encourage Josh and give him an overwhelming sense of Your presence and pleasure in his life. Help him as he trusts You and honors his boss. We pray these things in Jesus name. Amen."

Josh    "Thanks, that really means a lot to me."

Dan    "My pleasure! I'll continue to pray for you. I look forward to hearing what God does on your behalf in this situation."

## Debrief

As you listened to Dan's prayer for Josh, what impact did it have on you? In his prayer, in what way did Dan unleash a vision of God for Josh? In what ways did Dan's prayer model the values of keeping his prayer vertical, biblical and personal?

4. Break up into your spiritual partnerships. (Note: If your spiritual partner is absent, then partner with another same-gender person or turn a two-some into a three-some.) Quote Ephesians 3:20 for each other and ask each other what the Lord revealed to you as a result of meditating on this verse.

5. In your spiritual partnerships:

   a. One at a time, share something with your partner that warrants unleashing a vision of God for you through prayer. Ask each other, "What would you like to see God do in your life right now?" (This is not a role-play, but the real thing. It might be a challenge, problem, or decision you're facing.)

    b. Then pray for your partner unleashing a vision of God for them.

    c. After praying, ask the person you prayed for to share how this prayer unleashed a vision of God for them.

    d. Then switch off and reverse roles. Be sure to keep your prayers *vertical, biblical*, and *personal*.

6. Reconvene in your small group and debrief the above exercise maintaining confidentiality.

7. Discuss your responses to the questions you answered in preparation for this session.

8. Pray for each other using the guidelines for *conversational* prayer:

    ▪ Pray short, phrase or sentence prayers (Don't hog the conversation!)

    ▪ Listen to the Holy Spirit and each other

    ▪ Piggyback on each other's prayers. Stay on a theme until it seems right to move on

    ▪ Keep your prayers vertical (God-ward)

    ▪ Embrace silence as an opportunity to listen to God, transition to another topic, or process what has been prayed

    ▪ Believe the best of each other

9. Briefly go over the assignments for next week.

# CHAPTER 8

## Unleash a Vision of God through His Works!

**To prepare for this session:**

1. Read chapter 8 in *28:19 – The Skills for Disciple-Making* book.

2. Memorize Psalm 66:5 and meditate on it this week.

3. What was your biggest "Aha!" from reading this chapter?

4. Identify a work of God that unleashes a vision of Him for you and describe it here. (E.g., and example from nature, someone else's story or example, art, poetry, etc.)

5. What aspect of God's character or nature does this work of His reveal? What Scriptures support this?

6. Look for opportunities to unleash a vision of God through His works for someone this week and record your experience here.

## Group Session: Modeling and Coaching

This is the time you spend each week with whomever you are going through this Participant Manual (i.e., a spiritual partner, a small group, or a large group). If you are meeting as a large group with a small group element, please refer to the Tips in the box.

**Tips:** Address questions 1-3 as a whole group; conduct 4-7 in small groups; tackle items 8-9 in your spiritual partnerships allowing 15-20 minutes for this exercise; reconvene as a whole group for item 10.

By practicing the skills presented here you will model and coach each other in those skills with the goal of propelling each other into deeper relationship with Jesus Christ, resulting in a changed life. When you meet together:

1.  Open in prayer thanking the Lord for His presence among you. Pray expecting God to work in your midst and invite Him to continue to change you making you more like Christ.

2.  Be attentive to opportunities to pray for each other on the spot.

3.  Conduct the following simulation:

## Simulation

Jake and Tom are camping. For the past couple of hours they have been sitting around the campfire talking. Jake has been dealing with a lot of issues lately, including being fired from his job, tension with his spouse over that, and as if it couldn't get any worse, his car was stolen last week! The bottom line is that Jake is struggling with whether God really loves him.

Although it has been dark for hours, the fire has been so bright and the conversation so intense that neither had noticed the night sky. As the fire has dwindled to dimly glowing coals, both look up and stare up at the sky in complete awe.

Tom     "Can you believe the sky? I've never seen so many stars!"

Jake     "Yeah, and they're so bright! There's the Big Dipper, and the North Star on the Little Dipper." (Pause: both are just staring at the sky in wonder.)

Tom     "I heard a physicist speak one time and he said that there are so many stars, that if you set the most powerful computer in the world to counting them, computing as fast as it does, it would take the computer billions of years to count them all!"

Jake     "I can't even begin to imagine the power and the knowledge and the creativity that God wielded in creating the universe!"

Tom     "You got that right! As immense and complex as this all is, God is infinitely greater and more magnificent! In Psalms it says, "He determines the number of stars and calls them each by name."

You know, in view of God's amazing creation, I can't help but think about your current situation. (*Very caringly*) If God called all this into being by speaking a word, just think of what He can do for you in your situation! And if He knows the stars by name, think about how much more He cares for you, Jake!"

How did Tom unleash a vision of God for Jake? What might this action do for Jake in his situation?

4. Quote Psalm 66:5 for each other and tell each other what the Lord revealed to you as a result of meditating on this verse.

5. Ask each other, "How has God been revealing His great love for you lately?"

6. We were asked to identify a work of God that unleashes a vision of Him for us and describe it. What aspect of God's character or nature does this work of His reveal? What Scriptures support this?

7. Share what happened when you unleashed a vision of God for someone through a work of His?

8. Break into your spiritual partnerships and complete the following exercise, so that you both have the opportunity to unleash a vision of God for each other, one at a time. You may employ one or more of the four Actions for unleashing a vision of God in this exercise—through your story, through God's Word, through prayer, or through His works.

**Exercise**

Role A     Answer the question, "What is the most significant challenge you are facing in your life right
now and what makes it so weighty?"

Role B     Based on Role A's response to the above question, unleash a vision of God for them using one
or more of the four Actions for this Skill.

Debrief     In what way did Role B unleash a vision of God
for you and why was it effective?

Now switch roles and repeat the exercise.

9. Pray for each other using the guidelines for
*conversational prayer:*

- Pray short, phrase or sentence prayers
(Don't hog the conversation!)

- Listen to the Holy Spirit and each other

- Piggyback on each other's prayers. Stay on a theme
until it seems right to move on

- Keep your prayers vertical (God-ward)

- Embrace silence as an opportunity to listen to God,
transition to another topic, or process what has
been prayed

- Believe the best of each other

10. Briefly go over the assignments for next week.

# Courageously Challenge Others from God's Word!

**To prepare for this session:**

1. Read chapter 9 in *28:19 – The Skills for Disciple-Making* book.

2. Identify three key insights from this chapter that you found particularly impactful.

3. Memorize 2 Timothy 3:16-17 and meditate on it this week.

4. Think of an issue or area of life in which you would like to be courageously challenged and write it down here. How might you courageously challenge yourself from God's Word on this issue?

5. Pray for an opportunity to courageously challenge someone using the Word and record here what happened.

## Group Session: Modeling and Coaching

This is the time you spend each week with whomever you are going through this Participant Manual (i.e., a spiritual partner, a small group, or a large group). If you are meeting as a large group with a small group element, please refer to the Tips in the box.

**Tips:** Address items 1-3 as a whole group; conduct 4-6 in small groups; tackle items 7-8 in your spiritual partnerships allowing 15-20 minutes for this exercise; reconvene as a whole group for item 9.

By practicing the skills presented here you will model and coach each other in those skills with the goal of propelling each other into deeper relationship with Jesus Christ, resulting in a changed life. When you meet together:

1. Open in prayer thanking the Lord for His presence among you. Pray expecting God to work in your midst and invite Him to continue to change you making you more like Christ.

2. Be attentive to opportunities to pray for each other on the spot.

3. Ask two individuals to role-play the following scenario. *(Women can substitute Shauna for Steve and Grace for Garrett.)*

## Courageous Challenge Simulation

| | |
|---|---|
| Steve | "Hi, Garrett, it's good to see you. How are you doing?" |
| Garrett | (*Preoccupied*) "Oh, hi. (*Angry*) I've been better!" |
| Steve | "I'm sorry to hear that. What's going on?" |
| Garrett | (*Angry & emotional*) "I hate my job! I've got a boss who seems to have it in for me. We had a big argument today about the way I handled a client. I got so angry, I thought for sure he'd fire me!" |
| Steve | "Were you able to make things right with your boss?" |
| Garrett | (*Still angry*) "No. I clammed up and just left." |
| Steve | "Garrett, I understand how you feel, but what would restore your joy in this situation?" |
| Garrett | (*Sarcastic*) "A different boss or a new job!" |
| Steve | "I know, but God is immeasurably bigger than your boss or situation. He can meet you right where you are. Could I read something for you that I read this morning in Colossians?" |
| Garrett | (*Breaking*) "Yeah, sure." |
| Steve | "Just a moment, let me find it here. (Searching on iPhone) Here it is. 'Since God chose you to be the holy people whom He loves, you must clothe yourselves with tenderhearted mercy, kindness, humility, gentleness, and patience. You must make allowance for each other's faults and for- |

give the person who offends you. Remember, the Lord forgave you, so you must forgive others. And whatever you do or say, let it be as a representative of the Lord Jesus, all the while giving thanks through Him to God the Father.'" (Colossians 3:12-13, 17 NLT)

Garrett   (*Broken*) "That says it pretty clearly doesn't it. I guess I need to go and ask his forgiveness for my behavior and my attitude."

Steve   "If I were you, I'd go back to him immediately!"

Garrett   "You're right. I need to see him right away."

Steve   "Let me pray with you and I'll call you this afternoon to see how it went with your boss."

## Debrief

In what way did Steve unleash a vision of God for Garrett? Why is it important to unleash a vision of God for someone before we courageously challenge them? How did Steve courageously challenge Garrett? How effective was it? What made it effective?

The example above is quite directive. How might Steve have courageously challenged Garrett in a less directive manner?

4.  In your small groups, quote 2 Timothy 3:16-17 for each other and tell each other what the Lord revealed to you as a result of meditating on this verse.

5. Ask each other, "What has God been revealing to you from His Word lately?"

6. What key insights from this chapter did you find particularly impactful?

7. Break up into your spiritual partnerships. In your preparation for this session, we asked you to identify an issue or area of life in which you would like to be courageously challenged. Taking turns conduct the following exercise: (Note that this is not a role-play, but the genuine article!)

**Exercise**

Role A    Share the issue or area of life in which you would like to be courageously challenged.

Role B    Unleash a vision of God for your partner using one or more of the Actions for unleashing a vision of God. Then follow up by courageously challenging them using the Word of God.

**Debrief**

Identify how this person unleashed a vision of God and courageously challenged you. How effective was this? What made it effective?

Now switch roles and repeat the exercise.

Consider these additional "jump-start" questions especially if you don't know what Scripture to use in courageously challenging someone:

- With what Scripture do you think God would courageously challenge you right now?

- What Bible passage speaks to the issue you're facing right now?

8.  Pray for each other using the guidelines for *conversational prayer*:

    - Pray short, phrase or sentence prayers (Don't hog the conversation!)

    - Listen to the Holy Spirit and each other

    - Piggyback on each other's prayers. Stay on a theme until it seems right to move on

    - Keep your prayers vertical (God-ward)

    - Embrace silence as an opportunity to listen to God, transition to another topic, or process what has been prayed

    - Believe the best of each other

9.  Briefly go over the assignments for next week.

# Courageously Challenge Others through Prayer!

## To prepare for this session:

1. Read chapter 10 in *28:19 – The Skills for Disciple-Making* book.

2. Work through Colossians 1:9-14 (Paul and Timothy's prayer for the Colossians) using the Equipped in God's Word model. In what ways did Paul and Timothy courageously challenge their readers through this prayer? How can you apply their example of a courageous challenge through prayer when praying for others?

Memorize Colossians 1:10 (note that this is part of Paul and Timothy's prayer) and meditate on it this week.

3.  Watch for opportunities this week to courageously challenge someone through prayer. Write down your experiences here as you apply this Skill and Action. Also, be vigilant to pray for people "on-the-spot" when they voice a need or concern.

## Group Session: Modeling and Coaching

This is the time you spend each week with whomever you are going through this Participant Manual (i.e., a spiritual partner, a small group, or a large group). If you are meeting as a large group with a small group element, please refer to the Tips in the box.

**Tips:** Address items 1-2 as a whole group; conduct 3-5 in small groups; tackle items 6-7 in your spiritual partnerships allowing 15-20 minutes for this exercise; reconvene as a whole group for item 8.

By practicing the skills presented here you will model and coach each other in those skills with the goal of propelling each other into deeper relationship with Jesus Christ, resulting in a changed life. When you meet together:

1. Open in prayer thanking the Lord for His presence among you. Pray expecting God to work in your midst and invite Him to continue to change you making you more like Christ.

2. Be attentive to opportunities to pray for each other on the spot.

3. Quote Colossians 1:10 for each other and tell each other what the Lord revealed to you as a result of meditating on this verse.

4. Briefly discuss your findings from your work on Colossians 1:9-14.

5.  Discuss what is meant by the statement: "The courageous challenge through prayer is a *follow-up* to a courageous challenge we've already given."

6.  Break up into pairs with your spiritual partner and launch into the following exercise.

## Simulations

Read the two simulations below. You will each assume a role in the simulations, one of you taking the role of the person in the first simulation and the other the second. Your spiritual partner will unleash a vision of God for you using one or more of the Actions for that Skill and then courageously challenge you. You may courageously challenge using the Word, but in any case, do so through prayer. Asking a powerful open-ended question may be a key to getting to the place where you can pray for this person with a courageous challenge. (I.e., "What do you think God wants you to do in this situation?") Debrief after each simulation.

## Simulation one

Just a few hours ago, you had a blowup with one of your neighbors. You tried to confront him in a kind way about not letting his dog poop in your yard, but he got very defensive and then hostile. Some ugly and harsh words were exchanged in what degenerated to a yelling match. You are still so angry at his unwillingness to be reasonable and at the things he said, that you can't think straight!

You feel convicted about what happened, but you also have a strong sense of justice about the issue and believe that your request was perfectly legitimate. You have come here to your friend to unload on him/her about your situation.

## Debrief

Identify how your spiritual partner unleashed a vision of God for you and courageously challenged you. How effective were these actions? What made them effective?

## Simulation two

Things have been in turmoil for you at work during the past few weeks. The organization you work for initiated across-the-board pay reductions two months ago. Everyone has been walking on pins and needles and looking out solely for themselves. Teamwork is non-existent and everybody's fuses have been short. Now rumors are flying that deep cuts will be made in headcount as well!

You find your job and the current environment extremely stressful. You've been putting in long hours and haven't slept well in weeks. You've had to start taking something to calm your stomach. You cannot afford to lose your job! You feel panicked and desperately out of control. You're meeting with your friend to get some sympathy.

## Debrief

Identify how your spiritual partner unleashed a vision of God for you and courageously challenged you. How effective were these actions? What made them effective?

7. Pray for each other using the guidelines for *conversational prayer:*

   - Pray short, phrase or sentence prayers (Don't hog the conversation!)

   - Listen to the Holy Spirit and each other

   - Piggyback on each other's prayers. Stay on a theme until it seems right to move on

   - Keep your prayers vertical (God-ward)

   - Embrace silence as an opportunity to listen to God, transition to another topic, or process what has been prayed

   - Believe the best of each other

8. Briefly go over the assignments for next week.

# Courageously Challenge Others by Placing a "Y" in Their Path!

## To prepare for this session:

1. Read chapter 11 in *28:19 – The Skills for Disciple-Making* book.

2. Memorize Galatians 6:1-2 and meditate on it.

3. Read either Philemon or 1 Samuel 25:1-35 and work through the Equipped in God's Word model. What is God revealing to you from His Word and how will you respond?

4. Ask God to reveal to you an area of your life in which you have had a recurring struggle (e.g., anger, gossip, impure thoughts, etc.) or a specific act or event from your past that haunts you, from which you would like confirmation of forgiveness and freedom from guilt. Or ask Him to reveal to you a positive trait or discipline you'd like to develop. (See Psalm 139:23-24.)

Do not get hung-up on looking for your deepest, darkest secret! We all have issues with which we struggle but rarely share with another person. Keep Galatians 6:1-2 in mind. Come to your next group session prepared to share this issue with your spiritual partner.

5. Take advantage of at least one opportunity to courageously challenge someone toward Christ this week by placing a "Y" in their path. Capture what happens here:

## Group Session: Modeling and Coaching

This is the time you spend each week with whomever you are going through this Participant Manual (i.e., a spiritual partner, a small group, or a large group). If you are meeting as a large group with a small group element, please refer to the Tips in the box.

**Tips:** Address items 1-3 as a whole group; conduct 4-5 in small groups; tackle items 6-7 in your spiritual partnerships allowing 15-20 minutes for this exercise; reconvene as a whole group for item 8.

By practicing the skills presented here you will model and coach each other in those skills with the goal of propelling each other into deeper relationship with Jesus Christ, resulting in a changed life. When you meet together:

1.  Open in prayer thanking the Lord for His presence among you. Pray expecting God to work in your midst and invite Him to continue to change you making you more like Christ.

2.  Be attentive to opportunities to pray for each other on the spot.

3.  Ask two volunteers to role-play the following simulation:

## Simulation

Craig   "Hi, Tom, how's it going?"

Tom   "Hey, Craig. It's goin' okay." (Spoken with sense of defeat)

Craig    "Come on, Tom, level with me. You don't sound well."

Tom    "Is it that obvious? Well, here goes. You asked for it! Dawn and I have been married for 15 years, but our marriage is hurting. We haven't been intimate for months. Morgan, our middle child, is struggling in school with disciplinary issues and poor grades. We're deep in debt and I hate my job! Dawn just got promoted, but her increase in pay is eaten up by what she spends on her wardrobe in her new management position. I just feel overwhelmed! All this junk is sucking the life out of me!"

Craig    "Wow! You weren't kidding were you? No wonder you're feeling overwhelmed. Where do you see God in all of what you're going through?"

Tom    "Great question. I don't know. He seems far away or disinterested."

Craig    "I've experienced times too when God seemed far away, but I know He's not disinterested in you! He tells us in His Word that He loves us even more than we can comprehend. Jesus reminded us, 'If you being evil know how to give good gifts to your children, how much more will your Father in heaven give good gifts to those who ask Him!'" (Matthew 7:11)

Tom    "Yeah, well...I'm not experiencing many of those 'good gifts' right now."

Craig    "Tom, if you were to ask God to do one thing in your life right now, what would it be?"

| | |
|---|---|
| Tom | "That's easy! I'd ask Him to help Dawn and me fix our marriage. I think if we were pulling together as one, we could slog through the rest of the junk." |
| Craig | "Are you willing to do whatever it takes to get your marriage back on track?" |
| Tom | "Yes, I am!" |
| Craig | "Good! Then, I'm going to challenge you to do three things. First, how often do you pray with Dawn?" |
| Tom | "Occasionally at mealtime, but otherwise, not at all." |
| Craig | "Okay. I'm going to ask you to pray with Dawn aloud every day, sometime during the day. In your prayer, thank God for her and all she does. Ask God for wisdom, for His provision and help with all your other issues. Invite Jesus Christ into all that's going on in your lives. That's the first thing. |
| | Second, tell Dawn you love her every day at least once and demonstrate your love by listening to her, esteeming her, and serving her in ways beyond your current routine. That might be washing the dishes, vacuuming, whatever. If you can do something in particular that you know she does not like to do, that's all the better! Do it cheerfully and willingly. |
| | Third, meet with me once a week so we can pray together, get in the Word, and celebrate what |

God's doing in your life. Can you commit to those three things?"

Tom    "Yes, I can. I'll do it."

Craig    "Great! I'm excited for you and what God is going to do in your life! Can we meet each week here at this time?"

Tom    "Sure, that'll work."

Craig    "Also, may I call you tomorrow evening to see how you're doing on the first two challenges?"

Tom    "Sure. You're not going to let me off the hook on this are you?"

Craig    "No, I'm not, because I care about you and Dawn! Let me pray for you before you go.

Father, thank You for Tom's desire to draw closer to You and to his wife, Dawn. We pray that You would work in Dawn's heart to be receptive and responsive to Tom as he seeks to pray with her each day and love her in tangible ways. Lord, give this couple a renewed love for You and each other. Give them a fresh joy in their marriage. We pray too that You would work powerfully in Morgan's life and give her a desire to excel in school. Please meet Tom's needs at work and provide for them as they dig themselves out of debt. Strengthen, empower, and encourage Tom as he follows You in these things. In Jesus' name we pray, amen."

"I'll call you tomorrow evening then."

**Debrief**

- What did Craig do to determine where Tom was spiritually?

- How did Craig use Tom's words when challenging him and why was this important?

- How did Craig unleash a vision of God for Tom?

- What great open-ended question did Craig ask Tom to courageously challenge him by leading him to a decision to follow Jesus in this matter?

- Describe Craig's courageous challenge to Tom. Which Actions did Craig employ to courageously challenge him?

- Craig's courageous challenge was very direct in this example. How might Craig have courageously challenged Tom less directly?

4. Quote Galatians 6:1-2 for each other and tell each other what the Lord revealed to you as a result of meditating on this verse.

5. Take a few minutes to debrief the passage that you tackled this week using the Equipped in God's Word model (either Philemon or 1 Samuel 25:1-35).

6. Break into spiritual partnerships and work through the following exercise. In preparation for this session, we requested that you ask God to reveal to you an area of your life in which you have had a recurring struggle (e.g., anger, gossip, impure thoughts, etc.) or a specific act or event from your past that haunts you, from which you would like confirmation of forgiveness and freedom from guilt. Or ask Him to reveal to you a positive trait or discipline you'd like to develop. (See Psalm 139:23-24.)

   We encouraged you not to get hung-up on looking for your deepest, darkest secret! We all have issues with which we struggle, but rarely share with another person. Keep Galatians 6:1-2 in mind.

   Please take turns sharing with your spiritual partner whatever the Lord put on your heart. After your spiritual partner shares, please unleash a vision of God for them using one or more of the Actions for that Skill. Then, courageously challenge them toward Christ by placing a "Y" in their path. Finally, pray for your spiritual partner with a courageous challenge.

   Debrief between each round: In what way did your spiritual partner unleash a vision of God for you? In what way did your spiritual partner courageously challenge you? How effective was this for you? What will you differently as a result?

7. Pray for each other using the guidelines for *conversational prayer:*
   - Pray short, phrase or sentence prayers (Don't hog the conversation!)

- Listen to the Holy Spirit and each other

- Piggyback on each other's prayers. Stay on a theme until it seems right to move on

- Keep your prayers vertical (God-ward)

- Embrace silence as an opportunity to listen to God, transition to another topic, or process what has been prayed

- Believe the best of each other

8. Briefly go over the assignments for next week.

CHAPTER 12

# Courageously Challenge Others by Celebrating Their Personal Victories!

**To prepare for this session:**

1. Read chapter 12 in *28:19 – The Skills for Disciple-Making* book.

2. Memorize Philippians 1:6 and meditate on it.

3. What was your biggest "Aha!" from reading chapter 12 in 28:19?

4. Between now and the time you meet for your next group session, seek to courageously challenge someone daily by celebrating their personal victories. Record what happens.

5. Look back over the past 13 weeks.

   a. In what ways has God changed you?

   b. In what ways has God challenged you and propelled you forward in your relationship with Christ?

   c. In What ways do you feel you know God better as a result of this training?

   d. In what ways are you modeling Christ's transforming power in your life today?

   e. In what ways are you unleashing a vision of God for others?

   f. In what ways are you courageously challenging others toward deeper relationship with Jesus Christ?

g. In what ways do you purpose to continue to build and hone these Skills for Disciple-Making?

6. Pray about continuing your spiritual partnership after this training is over. Discuss this possibility with your spiritual partner.

*Since this is the final session of 28:19, you may wish to celebrate afterward by sharing a meal or snacks, but be sure to allot sufficient time for the various exercises and discussion as well.

## Group Session: Modeling and Coaching

This is the time you spend each week with whomever you are going through this Participant Manual (i.e., a spiritual partner, a small group, or a large group). If you are meeting as a large group with a small group element, please refer to the Tips in the box.

**Tips:** Address items 1-2 as a whole group; conduct 3-5 in small groups; tackle items 6-7 in your spiritual partnerships allowing at least 20 minutes for this exercise; reconvene as a whole group for items 8-10, allowing at least 30 minutes for this exercise.

By practicing the skills presented here you will model and coach each other in those skills with the goal of propelling each other into deeper relationship with Jesus Christ, resulting in a changed life. When you meet together:

1. Open in prayer thanking the Lord for His presence among you. Pray expecting God to work in your midst and invite Him to continue to change you making you more like Christ.

2. Be attentive to opportunities to pray for each other on the spot.

3. Quote Philippians 1:6 for each other and tell each other what the Lord revealed to you as a result of meditating on this verse.

4. In your small group, ask for a volunteer to role-play one of the following scenarios.

### Jon

A young man you know comes to you explaining that he has gotten his girlfriend pregnant. He seems genuinely repentant and deeply ashamed, not just because she is pregnant, but because of their immoral behavior. He tells you he wants to do the right thing and asks for prayer.

### Annie

Annie recently graduated from an out-of-state college and returned home. For the past two years she's been living with her boyfriend, Bret, but he broke it off just before graduation. Now she's back in town and nothing is the same. She's not motivated to pursue a job or to do much of anything. She really thought that she would marry Bret. She's all torn up inside. On the one hand, she feels used and abandoned, and on the other hand, she aches to be with him again.

Then ask the group the following questions:

    a.  How might we unleash a vision of God for Jon/Annie?

    b.  How might we courageously challenge Jon/Annie?

5.  Share your responses to question 5 that you completed in preparation for this session. Look for opportunities to unleash a vision of God and courageously challenge each other.

6.  Break up into your spiritual partnerships and role-play the following exercise with each other. (Men, use the case studies for men, and women, use those designed for women.) Take turns playing the role of the discipler and the role of the individuals represented here. When it's your turn to disciple, please use one or more of the four ways to celebrate the personal victories of the person presented in the case study. Use both case studies for this exercise.

**For men**
**John:** John is a man you have been meeting with for several weeks and he is gaining victory over outbursts of anger toward his wife and children. He has totally denounced this practice in his life and for the past two weeks he has been completely free of such outbursts. His freedom comes as a result of a moment-by-moment abiding in Christ.

**Ted:** Ted has experienced total transformation in his marriage over the past three months. Before that, he and his wife had been separated for a year and not on speaking terms. He is now demonstrating a sacrificial love for her and is learning to live with her in an understanding way. He is definitely on an upward trajectory in his marriage.

**For women**
**Tanya:** Tanya is a single woman that you have been meeting with for the past several weeks. She is gaining victory over an addiction to prescription drugs. She had been using the drugs to anesthetize herself against loneliness and

feelings of worthlessness. She has also made huge strides in trusting God as her heavenly Father and receiving her self-worth from Him.

**Julie:** Julie grew up in a Christian home, received Christ as a child and has called herself a Christian all her life. When you started meeting with her three months ago, she was totally disillusioned with Christianity and was carrying a lot of religious baggage. Julie is now totally in love with God! She is learning more and more each day about what it means to truly enjoy Him and abide with Him!

**Debrief the exercise:**
In what way did your spiritual partner choose to celebrate your personal victory? How effective was it? Why was it effective?

7. With your spiritual partner, come to a mutual agreement about whether to continue your spiritual partnership after this training ends.

8. While this concludes the formal experience of 28:19, the point is that we continue to use these disciple-making tools in our everyday lives from here on out.

   a. What have been some of the key areas of growth for you personally during 28:19?

   b.  In what ways are you implementing the skills for disciple-making in the lives of others?

   c.  What do we do in order to continue to develop these skills, applying them in our everyday lives?

9.  In view of what you shared with each other above, pray for each other using the guidelines for *conversational prayer:*

- Pray short, phrase or sentence prayers (Don't hog the conversation!)

- Listen to the Holy Spirit and each other

- Piggyback on each other's prayers. Stay on a theme until it seems right to move on

- Keep your prayers vertical (God-ward)

- Embrace silence as an opportunity to listen to God, transition to another topic, or process what has been prayed

- Believe the best of each other

10. Courageously challenge each with the following passage:

*Then Jesus came to them and said, "All authority in heaven and on earth has been given to me.19 Therefore go and make disciples of all nations, baptizing them in the name of the Father and of the Son and of the Holy Spirit,20 and teaching them to obey everything I have commanded you. And surely I am with you always, to the very end of the age." (Matthew 28:18-20)*

# SUPPLEMENTAL ROLE-PLAYS FOR ADDITIONAL PRACTICE

With your spiritual partner, one of you assume the role of an individual below and simply read your story (role-play) to your partner. Partners, listen with empathy and pray for God's leading in how to unleash a vision of God and courageously challenge your partner. Then debrief the exercise using the questions below.

## Fred

I'm a single guy in my late fifties. I've been divorced twice. I have two grown children by my first marriage. They are both single. My son lives in Florida and my daughter in New York, so I don't see them much anymore. I had a good job and worked hard all my life so I was able to retire a couple of years ago. Materially, I have everything I need or want, but I have no one to share it with. My life is the pits!

I received Christ as my Savior when I was a kid, but I haven't been very active in my faith.

## Tina

I'm a single mom with two small children. My husband abandoned us for another woman shortly after our youngest was born. I have a pretty good job, considering my training, or lack of it, but I still struggle even to make our rent and car payment, much less having funds left over for food and clothes for my kids. My oldest child is chronically ill, so I'm constantly missing work and spending money on doctors and medicine. I received Christ as my Savior a couple of years ago and I'm trying to have faith in Him and His care for me, but I don't know how much longer I can hang on like this!

## Tom

My wife and I have been married for 10 years, but we haven't been intimate for the past 18 months. We have three children. Our middle child is really struggling in school with disciplinary issues and poor grades. We're in deep debt and I hate my job. My wife just got promoted, but her increase in pay is eaten up by what she spends on her wardrobe in her new management position.

My wife and I both came to Christ when we were young and we still make a show of it by going to church. But somehow our Christianity is just not relevant to our situation.

## Karen

My husband and I have been married for 10 years, but we haven't been intimate for the past 18 months. We have three children. Our middle child is really struggling in school with disciplinary issues and poor grades. We're in deep debt and I hate the fact that I have to work outside the home. My husband just got promoted to a management position, but we're making less now than when he was hourly and could work overtime.

My husband and I both came to Christ when we were young and we still make a show of it by going to church. But somehow our Christianity is just not relevant to our situation.

**Role-Plays** *(continued)*

**Greg**

My wife and I have been married for 12 years and she just found out about an affair I had six years ago. My wife is devastated. Our marriage is crashing in around us. I don't know whether it will survive. My kids look at me as though I were the scum of the earth.

I have been a Christian since I was 15, but it doesn't seem to have helped much!

**Elaine**

I'm 47 years old. I received Christ as my Savior when I was 19. My walk with God has been filled with highs and lows ever since. There have been times for me of great elation in the Lord and other times when it seems that my prayers do not penetrate the ceiling. I have also experienced extended periods of great loneliness. In these times, I find myself questioning how God can love me and whether I'm even saved.

**Debrief simulations**

■ What actions did you use to unleash a vision of God and courageously challenge this person?

■ In what ways was your partner's unleashing a vision of God effective in your life?

# LIFESTYLE BENCHMARK

_____ is participating in a discipleship program. One of his/her projects is to ask several people that know him/her to complete this survey.

- ▪ Please answer the questions below by circling the most appropriate response.

- ▪ To ensure confidentiality, please DO NOT put your name on this survey.

- ▪ Please return this survey to this person within three days in the envelope provided.

- ▪ Please respond to the questions based on your knowledge and experience with this person.

- ▪ Leave a question blank only if you do not know this person well enough to respond accurately.

1. Even when no one is looking, this person strives to do his/her best while working on any task.

_Disagree_      _Disagree somewhat_      _Agree somewhat_      _Agree_

2. If this person inadvertently walked out of a store with a candy bar without paying for it, but in the parking lot realized his/her error, he/she would go back into the store and pay for the candy bar.

_Disagree_      _Disagree somewhat_      _Agree somewhat_      _Agree_

3. This individual would show compassion and respect if approached by a homeless person.

*Disagree*     *Disagree somewhat*     *Agree somewhat*    *Agree*

4. Even if presented with blatant temptation, this person would maintain sexual purity and moral self-control when traveling away from home.

*Disagree*     *Disagree somewhat*     *Agree somewhat*    *Agree*

5. This person is equally genuine in private as well as in public.

*Disagree*     *Disagree somewhat*     *Agree somewhat*    *Agree*

6. This person usually exhibits a joy in life that transcends his/her circumstances.

*Disagree*     *Disagree somewhat*     *Agree somewhat*    *Agree*

7. This person could help others wrestling with spiritual issues.

*Disagree*     *Disagree somewhat*     *Agree somewhat*    *Agree*

8. This person would keep his/her cool if someone abruptly cut them off in traffic.

*Disagree*     *Disagree somewhat*     *Agree somewhat*    *Agree*

9. If this individual overheard a destructive rumor about another person, he/she would not spread this rumor to others.

*Disagree*     *Disagree somewhat*     *Agree somewhat*    *Agree*

# MY STORY

LUKE 11:1-4

Luke 11:1-4

# OTHER BOOKS BY ROB FISCHER

*On Alert! – Staying Vigilant through Prayer*
*(Summit Leadership Series for Men)*

*Fully Equipped – God's Word: One of the Essentials for*
*Survival (Summit Leadership Series for Men)*

*Solitude – Spending Time Alone with God*
*(Summit Leadership Series for Men)*

*Comrades in Arms – The Power of Pursuing Christ in the*
*Company of Other Men*

*Rogue Principles that Grow Church Community* – A small
group curriculum and companion book to the movie *Rogue*
*Saints*

*Enthralled with God, 2nd Edition with Discussion Questions*

*Becoming Tarzan* – A humorous collection of childhood stories
that appeal to the whole family

*13 Jars* – The true stories of women who found redemption,
forgiveness and peace through Jesus Christ following their
abortions

*Drazenovich—An Alaskan Adventure* (historical novel)


Be sure to watch for other books coming in the
*Summit Leadership Series for Men!*

To contact Rob about his books or for coaching
visit him online at:
**www.fischerleadershipcoaching.com.**

## AUTHOR'S BIO

**Rob Fischer** has been discipling others for over 40 years. He has served on the staff of five US churches and helped establish two churches in Austria. God used Rob's passion and gifting to help these churches grow dramatically in discipleship and experiencing community.

Additionally, Rob leveraged his expertise within two major corporations struggling with toxic and dysfunctional behaviors and helped usher in a more positive work environment. Rob is an author and a leadership coach helping people discover God's vision for their lives and live accordingly.

Rob has been married to Linda for over 40 years. They enjoy three married children and ten grandchildren.

Made in the USA
Middletown, DE
23 January 2023

22899261R00066